Pathways to Early Literacy Series:
Discoveries in Writing and Reading

How
Very
Young
Children
Explore
Writing

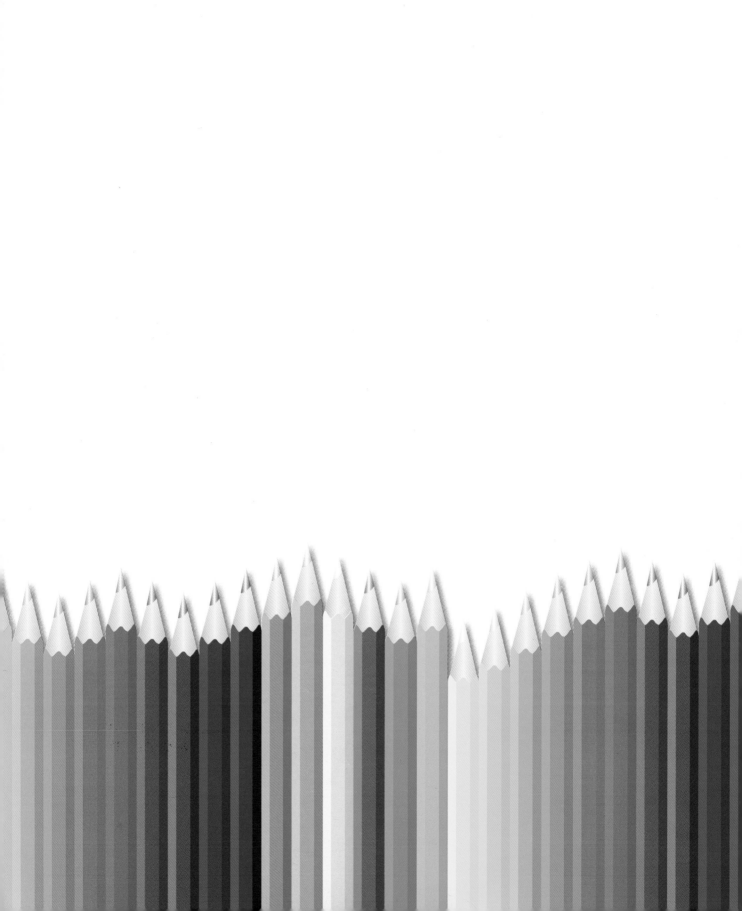

How Very Young Children Explore Writing

One in a series of books for parents, caregivers, and teachers of preschoolers and new entrants

Heinemann

Marie M. Clay

Cover photograph: Gladskikh Tatiana (Shutterstock Images)

Every effort has been made to trace and acknowledge copyright. However, should any infringement have occurred, the publishers tender their apologies and invite copyright owners to contact them.

www.pearsoned.co.nz

Your comments on this title are welcome at
feedback@pearsoned.co.nz

Pearson
a division of Pearson New Zealand Ltd
67 Apollo Drive, Rosedale, North Shore 0632, New Zealand

Associated companies throughout the world

Printed in Malaysia via Pearson Malaysia (CTP-VVP)

Editor: Mary Anne Doyle, Ph.D., Professor, University of Connecticut and Consulting Editor, The Marie Clay Literacy Trust
Text and cover design: Cheryl Rowe, Macarn Design

Library of Congress Cataloging-in-Publication Data
Clay, Marie M.
  How very young children explore writing / Marie Clay.
    p. cm. — (From the pathways to early literacy series)
  ISBN-13: 978-0-325-03405-8 (pbk. : alk. paper)
  ISBN-10: 0-325-03405-2 (pbk. : alk. paper) 1. English language--Composition and exercises--Study and teaching (Elementary). 2. Report writing--Study and teaching (Elementary). 3. Language arts   (Elementary).
  I. Title.
  LB1139.5.L35C544 2010
    372.62'3—dc22
                                    2010017450

United States: Heinemann, 361 Hanover Street, Portsmouth, NH 03801-3912.

The editors and publishers thank the following individuals for their assistance with this book: Billie Askew, Christine Boocock, Dorothy Churchwood, Jann Farmer-Hailey, Patricia Kelly, Rosalie Lockwood, Carol Lyons.

The pronouns 'she' and 'he' have often been used in this text to refer to the teacher and child respectively. Despite a possible charge of sexist bias it makes for clearer, easier reading if such references are consistent.

Contents

Series overview

This book is one in a series of three written for parents, caregivers, early childhood teachers, and teachers of children in their first year at school. No set order is intended. Each book offers unique discussions and suggestions, and each can be read independently; it is complete in itself.

How Very Young Children Explore Writing introduces the reader to the fascinating writing attempts of preschool children.

What Changes in Writing Can I See? introduces ways of keeping records of early writing. It describes how easy it is for parents and teachers to assess the changes taking place in children's writing by using everyday observations and by making more formal assessments.

The Puzzling Code discusses how puzzling the written code is for young learners beginning formal reading instruction and offers instructional recommendations for supporting the child's complex learning.

A preschool teacher comments on a young child's writing:

> *I thought it was just scribble. But it isn't — if you understand what it is you are looking at!*

This teacher is correct. If you understand a little about what the child is trying to do when he writes, you can celebrate with him and tempt him to explore a little more about writing. Why is this helpful? Any of a preschool child's early attempts to write, however slight or fragmentary they may seem, are very beneficial for his ongoing literacy development. The child who experiments with writing before he goes to school has the opportunity to discover new concepts and ways to express ideas in print. Praise from an observant adult encourages him to keep extending his new-found ability. This freedom to make trials and errors with adult approval is the best preparation I know of for learning to read and write proficiently in school.

An introduction to the series: My perspective on relevant issues

Early writing experiences

My perspective is that children's early writing experiences provide them with powerful learning opportunities that support the reading and writing instruction they will encounter once they enter school. As they write their earliest messages, children gradually begin to make links between speaking, reading and writing. They may discover that:

> What I say, I can write. And, what I write, I can read.

In the process of writing, they also learn many concepts about written language. For instance, they form understandings about letters and words, make connections between sounds and letters, and learn how to move left to right across the page. These discoveries are more beneficial to literacy learning than singing the alphabet or parroting rhymes about letter sounds. This raises the question of what is the place of phonics in reading instruction for our youngest learners.

When children begin to write little messages, lists, and other snippets of writing, parents often wonder whether they should teach phonics, or letter sounds, at home. I ask parents to just not buy into that idea. Think about it. In the phrase 'the phonics fad' what sounds do the letters 't', or 'h,' or 'p' have? What sounds would be the correct responses for each of the letters 'a, e, i, and o' in that phrase? Most English letters are used for more than one sound, so my questions are very confounding. When something happens often in a language, we think of it as a rule; however, many letter-sound correspondences in English break the rules, and that is very confusing for young children.

I agree that a reader has to learn to relate the sounds he speaks to the visual symbols of the writing system, but I assert that for the preschool child there is no better place to start than by helping him to write his personal messages. What I explain in this series of books is that instead of trying to teach children rules about our language (rules which are right only part of the time), we encourage them to speak their messages aloud (making the sounds), and we help them to write these messages.

Whenever I see or hear the advice 'you must teach your child phonics to prepare him to be a reader', I am reminded that this call has returned to education five times in my long life — twice during my school years and in three movements since then! Each time, phonics has been rejected as the royal road to reading because it doesn't take care of half of what the young child needs to know. Links between letters and sounds are very important, but a good literacy programme teaches much more. *Attending to the sounds made by letters in a word is a valuable but small part of what a reader has to know.*

At school, children begin the long task of linking the sounds (what they say) with the symbols (letters). Very quickly, they get the idea that there are regularities in letter-sound correspondences and the order of letters in words they read and write. But they also meet many irregularities when the 'rule' does not work.

One particular task that children do have to learn is how to listen to single sounds in the flow of their speech. This is a difficult task as individual sounds within words are quite hard for a young child to hear. Psychologists and linguists call this learning 'phonemic awareness.' To locate a particular sound in your own speech means learning to 'hear' one small piece of a larger speech pattern. Only then can you link the sounds to squiggles in print, the letters. Children take a couple of years to learn to hear the distinct sounds in what they say. However, once this learning is accomplished, they can hear most sounds, even the hardest examples, and the teacher's continued attention to phonemic awareness is not needed.

I have recently read well-designed research studies of advanced three- and four-year-olds who have taught themselves to read. The researchers show that these children could not pass the phonics tests commonly used by many school systems, and they did not 'sound out words' when they read. They have taught themselves to read *without learning phonics,* and researchers are still trying to find out how they do this. On the other hand, I know of no published research which shows that when any group of preschoolers has been taught 'phonics', it is the sole reason why they read well when they go to school. That belief is unsupported by evidence.

When we follow a very young child who is exploring print and trying to find out 'what is possible', we discover that he is trying to do something very complex. He starts by giving initial attention to the bits that are easy for him. Complex things are learned slowly, and each child shifts gradually from doing very simple things to doing very complex things. In young children's writing, it is that slow kind of learning, shifting week by week, that I advise parents and teachers to watch for, encourage and celebrate. It may not always seem easy to be the observer rather than the participant, but it is often in children's little, self-chosen spontaneous writing efforts that you can catch them in the act of discovery. That is when they are most likely to turn to you to share the joy of their achievements. There is no finer reward.

Individual differences resulting from early experiences

I have an unusual view of new entrants to school. They remind me of butterflies. Just as a butterfly emerges from a chrysalis, the school entrant is emerging from years of earlier development. He has learned to talk, and he has also seen print in his home and community. What each child chooses to attend to is very individual. Each arrives at school with his own set of understandings — his 'known'. This means that each child tends to know different things than other children about how we can write down what we say. A teacher cannot assume that all her children have similar understandings or knowledge. Each child's preschool literacy experiences and opportunities are personal and uniquely his own.

I take the view that instead of trying to teach children to work on small pieces of language, like letters and sounds, and a few words or sentence patterns, a good starting point is the child's own speech, its sounds, words, and sentence structures. He brings this knowledge to school. The task is to show him more about how his speech can be written down in new reading and writing tasks and how to expand speaking, reading, and writing outwards from there.

It is impossible to explain to young, preschool children how what we say is written down. The instruction and any directions from adults are beyond their understanding. You should therefore avoid trying to talk about it. Instead, chat about the purpose of your writing (the shopping list, the deposit form completed at the bank, the birthday card for grandad) and draw attention to the print around you in the home or the local environment (like stop signs and cereal packages). When you are writing, you can encourage children to join in the activity, like both writing a letter to grandma. You can also help them notice when people write and why they write.

Preschoolers today are aware of computers in the home and have often had experience in using them if only to play a computer game. They also may have watched older members of the family compose text messages or send emails. But this cannot take the place of learning to write. The activity of handwriting presents the two-fold challenge of physically forming the written letters and words as well as composing the messages in the mind. So it is vital that children also see adults engaging in handwriting for a variety of purposes. Above all, give children opportunities to make their own explorations in writing. If you can put together little writing kits of recycled paper of different kinds along with enticing pencils and crayons, and perhaps make a special space where the child can write at any time he chooses, you will channel his urge to write and need not worry about scribbles on the wallpaper!

I encourage you to be sceptical, critical, and thoughtful about any 'regimes' for teaching writing before school and any edicts about avoiding writing with preschool children. Instead, allow yourself to become fascinated by the ways a child's writing and his attention to print change through the years, particularly from age three to six.

How can adults support young children's attempts to write? This series of books provides an introduction to this fascinating topic, explores a variety of different approaches children may have to writing, and offers a range of recommendations.

1

Introduction to early writing

A little child who watches his parents or siblings make mysterious markings on paper will want to mimic their activity and 'be a writer' too.

There are many concepts about writing that children do not know when they first try to write. That does not put them off! They begin with small steps. Each step forward takes great effort. Ever so slowly they work at scribbling and making marks with some kind of writing tool on any paper they are given. Before long they seem to do, or understand, one or two of the following:

- They scribble.
- They find a shape in the scribble and repeat it over and over.
- They vary the size and shape of their marks.
- A letter appears and is repeated.
- Some letters have a right-way-up. Some letters don't.
- You can say, or name, a letter.
- Letters can make a pattern.
- People call the patterns words.
- You can find words in your 'talk' too.
- The order of marks in the pattern is important.
- The order of words in the message is important.

Everything in this list is critical. Yet it doesn't help one little bit to build these ideas into a sequenced curriculum for young children. Trying to teach preschool children these ideas is guaranteed to confuse them. The list is not a staircase. Different children will attend to any one of the ideas first and move to any other following their own ways and according to their own time schedules.

Children often surprise us. One of my great nephews suddenly bloomed as a writer, surprising his parents. About three weeks before his fourth birthday, he wrote T for Thomas. The next week he copied a recognisable 'Poppa' on a birthday card for his grandfather. Very soon after that, while drawing on his own, he wrote 'STOP' without help, asked his surprised mother if it said stop, then wrote 'GO,' and reread both. Two whole words! No teaching, no coaching, no obvious prior development! But, pause a minute to consider his experiences. These words were important and real signs he had used often as he played with his train engines and cars, and he had played with them for some time. He manipulated the signs, knew how to interpret them, and perhaps took a close look. Suddenly, in writing them on his own, he displayed some control over letter forms, letter order, and words, all at once.

Reconsider the list above and note that none of these early accomplishments have much to do with learning the letters of the alphabet. Be clear about this. The alphabet only puts the letters of a code into a particular order — it is a tiny, ready-reference gimmick. It helps older children and adults to locate information. The young child who learns to sing it, or say it, does not use the alphabet for what he is trying to learn. Thomas did not write 'STOP' and 'GO' because he knew letters of the alphabet; he acquired his known words from playing with his train set. From his repeated experiences during play, he became aware of these words. He focused on them and was able to remember them in detail.

What young children do with print is very interesting. When we watch the changes in their writing carefully, we see that what they are trying to do is simple at first but very quickly becomes complex. The examples in this book are for you to think about, but they are not things to make your child do. Consider how they suggest the emerging understandings that children acquire about literacy from their writing experiences. I hope you will marvel at how much children are able to learn about print before they are formally taught.

Most of us have forgotten how puzzled we were by language in print when we first tried to write. We got better and better, faster and faster until we have no memories left of what those first steps were like. Most adults think that looking at print is just something our eyes do, automatically, and something we never had to think about. Actually, we had to learn to do many things.

Parents and caregivers might think that perhaps we should hold back from encouraging children to write before entering school and leave attention to writing and print for teachers in classroom settings. Can parents do anything that would be helpful? Yes, they can be very helpful, and every preschool child has plenty of time to explore the way we put our language into print. Thomas at four has already made life easier for his first school teacher!

When babies are teething, you cannot predict when the first tooth will break through or how fast the other teeth will come in, or how beautiful the 'bite' might be at an older age. Similarly, with a child's first attempts to write, the precise timing of 'cutting his teeth' will be unpredictable.

The list of things I present above may be critical for learning to read and write, but children will come to understand them in any order and at any time between two and six years of age. There is no fixed sequence; much depends on experience and opportunity.

So, what can you do?

Work alongside a child and let him tell you what he is doing. Much of the child's early writing will be a joint effort with an experienced writer doing some of the work to get the younger one's message down on paper. At other times the child will just explore the possibilities of print and invent his own writing. Making marks, drawings, and scribbling will hold his interest briefly, and after a brief display of effort his attention will go to other things. Those brief moments of attention over the preschool years add up to quite important learning, preparing him for school. A special role for adults is to keep the child's interest alive and show enthusiasm for what he does.

I offer a special caution: *It is far too soon to aim for correctness.* Accept and enjoy the child's many attempts and accomplishments.

2

First there is scribble – ask yourself why

When you first look at a sample of a child's 'writing', ask yourself some questions about what you see. In the case of scribble it has something to do with finding out that he can make marks on some surface, no more and no less than that!

Children may begin scribbling at an early age, and they explore forms and shapes. Watch for circles, crosses, or a real letter.

These examples do not seem to represent the children's interest in recording messages. That is to be expected. Children enjoy playing with markers and paper and this activity leads to exploration and discovery, including the 'writing' of scribbled messages and eventually words.

Some children ignore writing altogether, and that does not matter; but if they do become interested, then early writing can change very quickly. And that's a great preparation for school! To introduce you to how far and how fast some children go in their exploring, we will look at a number of examples.

1 Primitive attempts

This is a television set. The little boy said so. Where did the letters come from? Not from his name. I did not see him do the drawing and writing. Just guessing is no good. We need to watch carefully and not jump to conclusions.

2 Inventing writing

Primitive forms (of letters and perhaps words) show up in the writing of most preschoolers. Those first attempts to write may be just the child's invention, as if he has not yet thought of copying print. Why do you think that happens? Is it easier to invent new marks than to copy something?

Consider the children's writing samples on page 14:

- Are these children making marks and exploring forms? Definitely!
- Do the marks stand for something? I can't tell — even though I can find several letter-like forms in their work (for example T, A, e, c, o, a, b, s, l, N, B, P, M, J, R).
- Do they expect the text to carry a message? I don't know. We have to ask the child.

Usually, the child is trying to make a shape he has made before, and he is not trying to copy letters or print. It is fun for him to explore because he finds new shapes. Watch for the first 'real' letter to emerge. Then wait patiently to see what emerges next! Let the child lead. That will avoid confusion.

3 Controlled, invented and varied

There's both control and inventiveness (playing around) in the next example.

'Well,' said Sally-Ann as she referred to her 'messages' within the circles, 'those are jokes for Dad!' She had been writing like this for some time. She ignored the lines on the page, rotated it, wrote across the paper, and drew in her own lines under her text. She seemed to make the circles for her 'jokes' before she thought of calling them jokes.

Another example shows Sally-Ann's flexibility. She appears to have found a way to make changes to her written words.

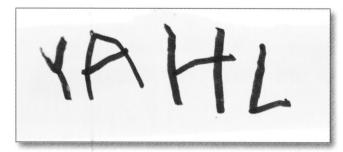

She began by announcing she would write some words. Starting at the top left of the page she wrote YA, and asked, 'What does that say, Daddy?'. Then she wrote I and asked again (YAI). Next she added marks to change the I into an H and wrote L ending with the word YAHL. Each time she added a letter, she asked her dad to read her word. Why did she do that? Perhaps she was wondering whether she had made a real word. Her dad did not read a real word, and discovering her efforts did not work, she gave up. We all give up when we cannot make the code work for us. In the process, she had discovered ways to produce a word and to make changes to a word.

If we could follow any of these children over a couple of years, we could watch how their writing changes. We would notice how and when they learn new things. It is not so important to determine when or whether the child is *correct*. Rather, when you see a change, it is important and interesting to ask yourself why this change has occurred.

The child's knowledge about writing gets shaken up every time he changes from a simple set of ideas to a more complex set of rules — the 'do' and 'do not' rules of our complex written code. A young child trying to write has to get his brain to do some challenging tasks, and all at the same time. More specifically:

- He must focus his eyes on the paper.
- He must get his hands to hold the pencil and the paper.
- He must move the pencil only in certain directions.

This is complicated! He stops. He checks. And he often goes back and tries again. These actions tell us that he is attending to 'how to do writing.'

At the same time these writing behaviours are emerging, it is not unusual for adults to attend to quite different challenges. They talk about letter names, and letter sounds, and how to make balls, sticks, and tails, and where to place the sticks to make certain letters correctly. A child who is trying to focus his eyes and control both his hands and the markers (for example, a crayon or pencil) will hardly notice what the adults are talking about. His attention is somewhere else — on the work he is trying to accomplish.

It is so easy for adults and children to be working at cross-purposes. To avoid that dilemma, let the child lead. Be patient: give up trying to teach something about letter formation and/or spelling while the child has to attend to finding spaces on the page and forming letters. He is intuitively putting first things first, and we are wise if we respect his judgement. Other learning will follow in its turn.

If adults make writing seem like hard work (and they often do), the child will quickly learn to avoid the writing task altogether. Guide the preschool writer gently, as you would a toddler learning to walk. Keep everything light-hearted and unpressured. Without talking about your demonstrations, invite him to imitate them. If you write, he will often mimic you and this can work very well. On the other hand, explaining what he *should* do may not work.

For preschool children, age is no indication of what should be learned, or what should be apparent in their writing. Before they go to school, young children are on their own time schedules for learning to write. Their interest may develop early, or it may develop late. This brings me to share the following strong hint: Rules, schedules, programmes, set sequences, and worksheets have little place in the early explorations of young children beginning to write. Spontaneity, and enthusiasm that ebbs and flows, are the characteristics of early childhood. Cherish these moments and celebrate the changes they bring about.

3   Pictures carry the story

Experience has shown me that some children may not exhibit the types of writing behaviours described earlier, preferring to draw. In many instances, these children who draw but do not write may still be on the way to writing as they show understanding of the connections between pictures and writers' messages by sharing their personal compositions. For a preschool child to understand these concepts is an important early accomplishment, one that will support early school writing and reading activities.

Child artists told their stories about the next three drawings. They clearly understand how stories and pictures are related.

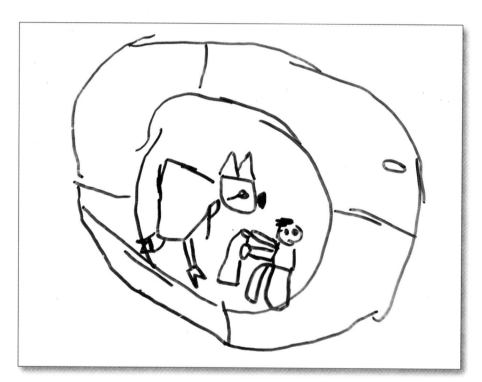

Mark's art was motivated by a matador story, but he adjusted it to fit his local school scene. He dictated the story for his teacher to write down:

'The boys play bulls and frighten the girls at playtime.'

Thomas's art and story were motivated by a personal experience and special intrigue in a rainbow he could see from his yard.

At four years of age, Thomas dictated the following story for his mother to write down:

'It is raining and the sun is shining and I see a rainbow. It's fun to play in the rain.'

Denise, at four and a half years, explains her picture and makes her message clear:

'This lady makes dolls. She has made those ones in the basket.
She is holding the hand of the one she is making.'

4 | When you write it gives the child ideas

Adults and older siblings in the home are the preschool child's first models of writing, and the child gains important understandings from opportunities to see and talk about writing with them. It is very beneficial for the parent to work alongside the child, sharing both the purposes for writing and the finished products (letters, bank forms, shopping lists). This exposes children to ways of recording messages (for example, in cursive writing) and the various forms writing might take. Opportunities for the child to add his message to a parent's written piece are also motivating and reinforcing.

In addition to these experiences, it is helpful for parents to point out print in the child's environment, including signs on the road or in shops, messages on cereal boxes, and letters from relatives and friends. The impact of the parent's help with and attention to their child's writing may be seen in the following samples.

Early writing is mostly scribble or a way of creating something like adult handwriting. Alison knows a few signs. She makes a good attempt at her name and then she 'does what grown-ups do' — cursive handwriting.

Shelby, at three years of age, chose to fill a whole paper with her writing; six lines, or streamers, of scribble. She also presents a good attempt at her name.

Margaux, age four years, had many experiences writing thank you letters with her mother. When her dad's wallet was found in the street by a neighbour, she was very pleased to write a thank you note. She wrote her note using a top to bottom, left to right orientation, and talked as she wrote each line. Her dictated message was:

'Dear Delia,
Thank you for
finding Daddy's wallet, and
thank you for my present.'

The interesting part of the message is that she had not received a present from Delia. It appears that her prior experiences with thank you notes related to expressing appreciation for gifts received. So this was to be part of her thank you message to Delia as well. She closed her note writing 'Love, MARGAUX'. She wrote each letter of her name in correct sequence, asking for models of R and G. Notice where she found space for her X, which is rotated and looks like a t.

Courtney, age five years, announced she was going to write a long story. She proceeded to fill her page by repeating familiar words, letters, and symbols. She even included an illustration. Courtney had enjoyed being read to by her parents and studied her many books. She seemed to acquire her sense of a full page of printed text, with an illustration, from this experience.

These examples suggest that the young writers have gained both awareness of using writing to express their thoughts and ways to present, or record, their intended messages. Their writing will change as they continue to explore and gain more control. It is informative to continue asking 'What is this child noticing now? What has he discovered?' Notice when the writing changes. Celebrate changes.

Has the child discovered something new or is it invention?

Children enjoy creating early messages. The task seems to have its own attraction if their efforts are encouraged and appreciated.

Nina was excited to send a letter to Santa telling him what she wanted for Christmas! To the reader this may look like she was inventing with limited control of letters and no words except her name, however, Nina's message shows that:

- She can convey her message in print
- Messages may take several lines of text.
- Her message is composed of words.
- Words are a collection of letters.
- Some letters are used repeatedly.
- She can sign her message with her name.
- She can spell and print her name correctly.

This is a beginning that demonstrates that Nina understands many concepts about conveying messages in print. As she continues to explore, she will discover more about letters and sounds and words, and ways to express her ideas in print.

Colleen's stories (opposite), written over several months, also demonstrate how a child's writing progresses. What are her discoveries?

Her early attempts at writing appear to be inventive, just a string of letters. She progressed to using letters that represented sounds she might hear or expect to see (second example), and then she demonstrated more control of letters and words and the ability to express a complete story independently.

For preschool writers, gross approximations become refined over time. Invented words, make-believe sentences, unusual letter forms give way to more conventional forms as the child discovers the principles of written language. Adults support this growth as they encourage young learners and provide many experiences to explore and write.

colleen

I am going trick-or-treating.

FYJH O O P

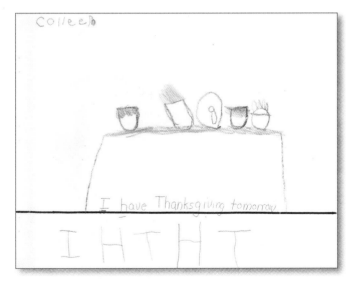

colleen

I have Thanksgiving tomorrow

I H T H T

I like Kashey
BEANut
Butter

How does the child use space on the page?

Print has space rules that drawing does not have. Look at how Harriet places writing on a page in the next example. Think about how Harriet used the space. Ask yourself why she did so? Does she know how to write on a piece of paper? What does she know about letters?

She drew her friend Raphaela and wrote both names. Her name is broken up and scattered around the page on the right hand side as she finds a space for each letter, but she made each one in the correct order. She used space creatively to record Raphaela as well. She printed each letter in correct sequence, wrote left to right and, running out of space after recording three letters (Rap), she returned to the left on top of the Rap to complete the name (writing haela).

Within a day or so her mother found that she had written her name clearly from left-to-right (see the example below). Her letter formation was not good, but the order of the letters was correct. If it was written from left to right, it was a terrific achievement. Notice something else: She has marked each with a red dot. Why would she do that? Perhaps this was her attempt to carefully check herself, a very important step.

Loren was about the same age as Harriet when she wrote her name. Look to the right of the next example. A casual observer might have arrived too late to see how the writing was done. Loren knew the letters of her name, in the correct spelling order. She wrote L, Lo, Lor, Lore, Loren. Her letter formation was not good, yet it would be easy to underestimate what she is able to do if we only looked at the final result.

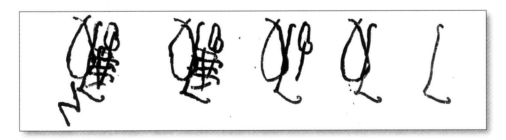

Getting control of letter-making takes time

Children are very flexible in their writing, varying their use of space on the page, the placement of letters to form words, and the orientation of letters (for example, rotated or inverted). Samples of writing presented on previous pages display these tendencies. (Note the signatures of Margaux, Harriet, Loren and Jonny.)

Jonny's writing also shows flexible use of space on his page, placement of letters, and the orientation of letters. He drew a picture of a football game (below), told his story about Kyle making a score, and added print to his picture. He made a very good attempt at writing Kyle and printed KYL right to left, reversing the L. Moving to the right of the name he printed, again from right to left, m, a, s. Jonny's oral story included the statement 'Kyle makes a score.' It appears that even though his use of space and

directionality demonstrate flexibility, or unawareness, we can deduce from his oral message that he did understand how to represent the initial sounds in words with success. This is a significant accomplishment for a preschooler.

Note that the goal is labelled LE (with an inverted L and reversed E). Again, he recorded the letters writing right to left (EL). Does it appear that he was recording what he could hear and represent in the word goal? Perhaps.

His signature was written bottom-to-top in a space he could find. Letters are sequenced correctly, but note his formation of the J and n.

In Nina's writing (below) we see a child who shows variability in directional movement and the orientation of letters in one writing sample. Examine DADDY (written left to right with reversed letters) and Dylan (written right to left)

I find that these various forms represent the preschooler's explorations of letter and word forms. Control will come with more experience. In general, if a child finds it difficult to make the movements correctly, his attempts to form letters will look big or heavy, sometimes good and sometimes not. Probably because copying is tedious the child shifts quickly to producing some letters without looking at the copy.

When you see the child making a careful decision about where to start a letter, or being anxious to correct mistakes in directional movement or in forming letters, that is great. It signifies that he has come a very long way in his learning. He has gained awareness of the directional principles that writers must adhere to. Drawing does not have those kinds of rules: writing does. He has gained important understandings that will help him in all literacy activities, both writing and reading.

A child's explorations in writing will result in numerous 'mistakes.' Try to avoid correcting. Just say something like: 'Oh yes, I can do that too.' Write for the child, but don't worry if he seems to ignore it. He may decide the task is too tough right now! That call is his to make. So the young writer adds detail and invents new things.

My words are my take-off platform

Thomas was just four years old. He talked well, loved trains, and kept himself busy with books, games, puzzles, and toy cars. His parents noticed that he drew circles and added a straight line touching the circle in different places, and he wrote T for Thomas. When his grandad, called Poppa, had a birthday, Thomas wrote a card for him. Poppa asked him to show what he could write. This is what unfolded.

He carefully constructed 'poppa' letter by letter, on request, left to right, ball and stick, circle, ball and stick, repeated, saying 'there are two P's.' He stopped and someone prompted 'You need another ...' 'A' he interrupted, and made a circle. He then added a short line to the right side saying, 'It's got a side there.'

He was then directed to write Thomas. He took a new sheet of paper and, moving right to left, he produced T, o, m, a (with a stick on the side) and s. He knew the order of the letters in his name from first to last. He also demonstrated awareness of three features of letters: a circle or ball, a small straight line or stick, and a snake that served for s and m.

Thomas had written the words 'Stop' and 'Go' a few days earlier, and he was prompted to write 'stop.' He began at the bottom of the page, making 's', an upside down 't,' an 'o' and a 'p' with a detached stick. He said, 'Stop'. His letters were not well formed, but he constructed a readable word from the few bits of the written code that he was able to juggle. Clearly, he tried to fit what he knew to what he was trying to do. He talked about it as he worked.

Looking at his word, 'Stop', he said to me, 'If you write it with a 'p,' it says pots.' He thought that was a huge joke that someone had told him although I don't think he understood why.

How could words suddenly appear like this? Thomas had had many encounters with the word 'stop' in his play. He had a stop sign for his train set, and it appears that he had tried to copy it. Because he began his copying by going right to left, he was cautioned by his parent that his word would not say 'stop,' but would then say 'pots.' What a joke, and one that he remembered even if he could not quite understand.

A milestone is reached when a child masters a word or two, often his, or someone else's name, and this will be long after he spoke his first word.

Writing one's name is a significant accomplishment, and I provide four examples: Nina, Matthew, Thomas, and Jonathan.

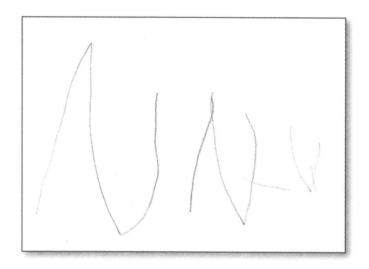

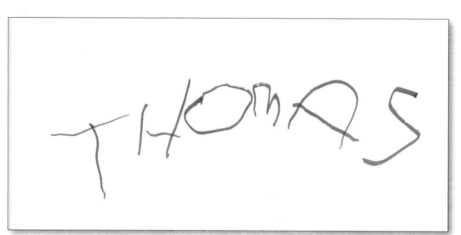

Every letter in Nina's name tells me that her hand is having a little trouble forming the letters. Matthew, Thomas, and Jonathan, a bit older, also write with some hesitancy. These children are not fluent in forming the letters, and they may have letter confusions, but all four are gaining important understandings. The child who can write his or her name begins to appreciate important features of a code, or written language. It is made up of special marks (letters), placed in a certain order, making a recognisable pattern. With this achievement, any one of a host of things may happen.

The child may learn to write a few known words. He may use any space on a page, scattering letters or words like confetti, but aspects (for example, letter order) will be correct. (Look back at how Loren or Harriet wrote her name on page 27, or Jonny's placement of letters in writing his football story on page 30.)

Pointing to the words more or less well, he may be able to read his own writing. He may ask for a copy of a new word to put into his message. He may learn, as Thomas did, that new words can be made from known words.

Remember if the job gets difficult or the child gets tired then he will go back to what is easier, and away from what might be harder. This is to be expected.

Moving across print involves strict rules

The way in which the English language is written down makes *no allowances* for handedness! Left-handed children and right-handed children must all move across print in the same left to right direction. All children find it difficult to get control of the correct movement. Drawing can go in any direction; writing cannot. In fact, there are many confusing things about direction in every language code. Here are six things the novice writer gradually learns:

- Don't print straight down the page.
- Don't write from right to left across a line.
- Don't snake back at the end of a line (going right to left).
- Don't go from bottom to top.
- Don't select a right page before a left page (when presented with open pages).
- Don't reverse any of the movements even though you find it easy.

You must be flexible and changeable when you are trying to print a message *except for the way you move across a page of print*. For that movement you must not be flexible.

The problem does not appear to be learning to move from left-to-right for printed English. The problem is to learn what NOT to do, because all but one of the possibilities is wrong! It takes quite a long time for young children to direct their attention and move left-to-right consistenty in reading and in writing.

All through his short life the child has been learning to manage himself in space. To move beyond scattering his writing around the page, he needs to feel the importance of the left side of the page, and the position of his body helps him to learn this. Ask yourself some questions about how this child moves:

- How well does he control his eyes, hands, and body?
- Does he have a feel for things to the left side and to the right side?
- Does he clearly approach print from the wrong side?
- Does his drawing or writing show any sense of directional rules?

Co-ordination and control of body movements are developing throughout the preschool years. Learning to approach print consistently from left to right has a lot to do with having good control over body movements.

A child about to go to school may point to print and pretend to read 'This is a fish,' or he may not. He may even write from left to right across a line. But watch him carefully as he reads or writes, or pretends to do those things. Where does he move to after reaching the end of the first line?

If the child goes left to right across the left page of a book, what does he do on the right page? That might take just a little longer to learn. Again, those things are related to how the child controls body movements, and bodies have their own schedules for getting that control.

After much exploring, the child discards all the wrong moves. He begins writing at the top left, moves left-to-right, and makes a return sweep repeatedly. It is a huge advance. But usually there will be some lapses, and this is to be expected.

Pretend you are reading the following two texts. One is in Hebrew and one is in Arabic. Scan the print from right to left. Pick up information from right to left. It is quite a hard task.

Sometimes the hands and eyes do not learn as quickly as the mind. Be patient with the young child.

Which way round does the letter go?

Yes, it does matter. A code is a code. It has to be done 'the right way.' But, turning letters around or making some error in letter formation may persist unnoticed by the child for some time. This may be seen in the way children write their names. Jenny for many months signed her name as Jehhy, and Jonny consistently reversed the J and printed his n like an h.

Other examples of reversed letters appearing in children's writing are found in the samples below: Jonathan's story (the letter a), Courtney's list of pets (b in rabbit), and Brian's lion (the letter n).

I lïke opplor.

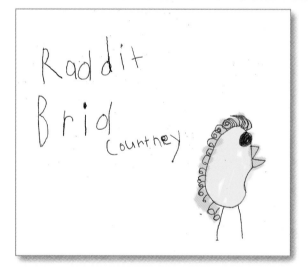

Raddit
Brid
Courtney

p liod

12 It gets more complex

Here are some great achievements observed in preschool children:

- He finds letters he knows inside words.

> At the age of three years, Matthew circled all M's in his grandmother's magazine.

- He points to a known word in a line of words.

> At the age of four years, Thomas located his cousin's name, Joy, in family Christmas cards.

- She can search a double-page spread in a book for signs she knows.

> Opening a storybook, Colleen found her known word *mum* on both pages of the open text.

- He notices the space between words and tries to use this in his writing. He will probably do it sometimes and forget all about it at other times.

> T h i s e l e p h a n t i s e a t i n g p e a n u t s. (*This elephant is eating peanuts.*)

- Knowing only a few letters, he pretends to make up different words. He can be flexible.

However, even with these accomplishments, if you were to talk about first and last letters and spaces between words, the preschool child would probably find it difficult. Take that kind of talk slowly.

Some children make short lists of 'words I know.' Those first words are the child's entry ticket to school learning. See Mark's inventory on the next page. Once the child is in school and paying daily attention to writing, the inventories grow longer very quickly.

At the end of the first year of school there are still challenges for Mark. Some of his letters (below) look just as good to him reversed or back to front. His teacher, who has observed Mark over the year, will know how to interpret this. Occasionally, known things in writing get neglected as the child tries new challenges. Perhaps Mark's reversals are a signal of new problem solving.

Children begin to play with words long before they know all their letters. They may begin to represent sounds with their known letters correctly, as Jonny did on page 30, demonstrating complex learning.

Often children begin to 'play safe' and compose their messages only from short words they know. You can encourage them to be more inventive with a comment like, 'You try it first.'

13 Many other signs and signals

Punctuation signs fascinate some young writers. Once discovered they pop up all over the place. These include:

- Period/full stop
- Question mark
- Quotation marks
- The 'excited' (exclamation) mark
- Apostrophe.

Decorative 'bits' add variety. However, the next example is not just decoration. It is a mixture of two written languages — an English word (below left) decorated with the 'curls' used in the Thai script (below right) by a bilingual five-year-old in the United States. It is as if she is signalling that she will have to print in both languages. She has them both in her head, so she combines them in her writing.

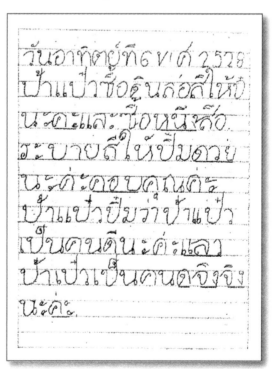

14 | Learning more letters

I am occasionally asked how many letters a child should know before entering school. One to five would be a start; the full set of 54 capital and lower case letters would be almost impossible. (This number includes 26 upper case letters, 26 lower case letters and two ways of writing 'a' and 'g'.)

Any letters would be helpful. They would be something to build on when formal instruction begins. The preschool child does not have a lot of use for certain letters. Let him build up knowledge of letters that is linked to what he wants to do, the words and messages he wants to write. This might include the letters in his first name or the letters in frequently-used words like Mum and Daddy.

Can you tell which letter he is making? He is sure to be confusing some; that's part of the learning game. Don't fuss about poorly-formed letters. Just keep popping in your own good shapes or models.

Remember anything new (including learning a new letter) could throw the child off a bit and old habits may suddenly reappear. With time and experience, these will disappear again and the child will be more secure in his 'known'.

It is important to understand that it is easy for letters that look a bit alike to become confused. Examples of easy-to-confuse letters include:

- e and a
- h with n and r
- k and y
- m and w.

When the child is able to notice the features of these letters and account for the detail of orientation, such confusions will disappear. That will take more time and experience. Preschool children sort such things out gradually.

15 | Finding letters in words

The activity of finding letters in words is powerful as it leads to word building. You may observe some of these things:

- He breaks individual letters out of words.
- He finds some letters that are easy to write, others hard.
- He finds a small word in a big word.

These accomplishments tell you that the child is looking closely at print and the features of letters and words. He shares his learning by using his current level of expression and understanding:

> *This word has no Stephens* (the letter S), *and this word has one Timmy* (the letter T).

> *This word* (pointing to Any) *is like my sister's name* (Amy). *But it's not right.*

> *I see 'and' here* (in sand) *and here* (in sandwich).

Or, he might comment when he expects one thing (based on his knowledge of spoken language) and sees another (from what he knows about writing).

These are not small accomplishments. These preschool children are gaining complex understandings from their writing experiences. In the world of codes this is quite an achievement.

Finding something a little more complex

Most new learning opens pathways to more interesting things about the language code. Children will slowly master:

- Recognising some capital and lower case letters in alternate forms (T, t).
- Hearing the first letter in a spoken word.
- Building a bundle of 'words I can write'.

They often want to make lists of letters, words, and numbers. They seem to search their brains for all the things they know.

The first few written words they learn are important. Once in school, the list will grow quickly. Look below at a bilingual Maori boy's May list of known words and compare it with his October list. You do not have to be able to understand his Maori words to see what great progress he has made. A small cluster of words you can write when you first go to school is a launching pad for learning to read and write. Don't push for a particular change just because you would like to see it.

Rauti's writing vocabulary in May.

Rauti's writing vocabulary in October.

17 One-to-one pointing is very clever

As the child tries to re-read what he has written, he may try to point to the marks on the paper. A young child learns to point to things one after the other — toys, spoons, buttons, coins in a line. If that is too hard for him, then he won't be able to think clearly about letters and words, one after the other, in writing. The child who learns to point to objects around him uses that one-to-one pointing to re-read his writing.

Some children will need support to successfully co-ordinate pointing, or locating, behaviours. Be available, interested and helpful by using appropriate props (toys, coins and so on) to help him establish pointing behaviours. Demonstrate what to do, remembering that an adult's talk about what to do is too difficult for him to understand. Support the child's attempts. With encouragement, he will be successful in time.

Forming a message and putting it down in print

Once in school, children will find that teachers question them about the stories they read. They want to check on whether the children understand what is written in print. We have a very easy way to gauge this. When a child writes a precise message which he wants us to understand, we can be fairly sure that his comprehension of how we communicate in print is developing.

The message in the next example is clear. This five-year old understands that writing is a way of sending messages.

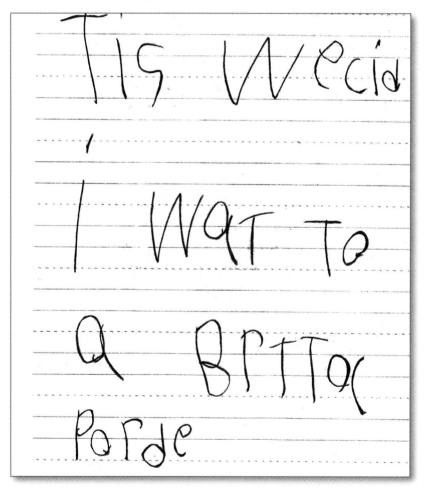

This weekend I went to a birthday party.

Once they get the idea of how print carries messages, they tell you what their written message says (even when it looks like nonsense), or they explain what they intended it to say (see Sally-Ann's jokes for Daddy, page 15). Perhaps they will ask adults to read the message aloud to check on it, but ultimately they begin re-reading what they have written to make sure the message is the one they intended.

We cannot deny it: Reading a message back is a child's check on whether the message was the one he was trying to send. Most people want to correct the child's spelling or check whether all the words are there. When I re-read my sentences as I write this book, I am also checking on whether the message can be understood. That is a comprehension check. Did I send the correct message?

The child who asks that question has, without doubt, established the first links between print and comprehending messages in print. Encourage children to explore and invent. Create openings for new things to be discovered.

Suggestions for parents, caregivers and preschool teachers

The following suggestions are intended to support parents, caregivers, and preschool teachers in the very special roles they play in the young child's path to discovery and writing. Children's early writing experiences provide them with powerful learning opportunities that contribute to their ongoing reading and writing progress. Children develop at their own rates and display unique trajectories, treading their own individual pathways to successful literacy achievement.

- The child wants to write. Act delighted!
- Provide pencils, markers, crayons, and papers in a place where children can use them, like near the doll's house or the toy train station.
- Forget all adult objections like 'messy', 'too hard', and 'too soon'.
- Remember that the child's question is 'What is possible?'
- Point to where he can write, or where he can start.
- Demonstrate how to do one simple thing.
- Help if the child will let you.
- Provide just the help the child asks for. Resist the temptation to go beyond his present need.
- Write yourself, alongside the child.
- Ask if you can keep the writing in a safe place. Date the writing sample.
- Watch how he works. Write down your observations.
- Make one important letter slowly (for example, the first letter of his name). He may learn something (or not).
- Talk about what you are doing while the child is watching.
- Write short words.
- Use lower case letters (not just capitals).
- Make time to be involved in his writing activity. Your interest will encourage him.
- Notice when his writing changes. Celebrate changes!
- Your child invents something new. Celebrate!
- Encourage children to explore and invent.
- Create openings for new things to happen.
- Provide clear examples, but accept rough copies with delight.

- Don't 'sell' children the correct way to write. Help them to discover that for themselves.
- Don't worry about teaching sounds or phonics.
- In the early stages, the hands do not learn as quickly as the mind does. Be patient as he begins to control his movements on paper.
- Create reasons for writing and show examples. Show interest and make writing fun.
- Try to avoid correcting. Say, 'Oh yes, I can do that too. Look!' And demonstrate.

I close with writing samples collected from children in their first years of school (ages 5–7 years). Their early experiences with supportive adults were very beneficial and contributed importantly to their literacy development over their first grade year. Note their strengths.

The first example is Michael's letter, written when he was about six and a half years old.

> Dear Mary,
> I have not bean reading the house at pooh corner but when I got your card I found the house at pooh corner and started reading the house at pooh corner, I am up to chapter 6. you now the card on the front tiger is forlling out of a tree I found that in the book to times on the back cover and in chapter 4.
> My arm is conpletley beter now exsepet I have to ecsesise if for 4 weeks.
> Michael

Michael sends a clear message in his letter; we can comprehend his meanings. There are 55 correctly-spelled words and some brave attempts at words that he has yet to learn, including bean (been), now (know), forling (falling), to (two), conpletley (completely), beter (better), exsepet (except), and ecsesise (exercise).

Courtney's letter to her dad, written when he was away on business, is the second example.

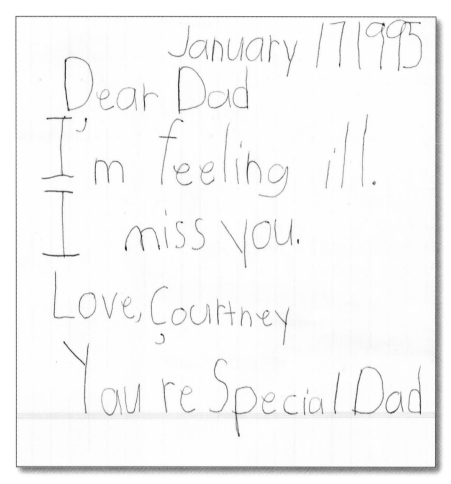

Courtney also sends a clear message. She is well aware of the form used for letter-writing, and is very accurate in her spelling (13/14 words written correctly). She also is aware of contractions and has only one incorrect attempt (Yau're for You're).

Finally, note Adrian's strengths as he explains why he does not need to write. Adrian was nearly six but he knew he could spell quite well: He was now old enough and competent enough to talk about his abilities. Younger children with less experience cannot do that.

Adrian	*I'm not going to write a story today.*
Teacher	*Why not?*
Adrian	*Because I want to read.*
Teacher	*But you write good stories and you learn to write lots of words.*
Adrian	*I can write all the words.*
Teacher	*OK, you tell me all the words.*

Adrian	*I am going to the shops with my mother and Cila is coming too and my Mother words in a factory* (pauses) *fac-tor-y* (pause) *and my father works in a bar. He gets lots of money for* (pause).
Teacher	*How do you write 'lots'?*
Adrian	*It's like 'got.' And, Cila is coming to school soon.*
Teacher	*How do you write 'soon?'*
Adrian	*It's got two 'Os.'*
Teacher	*Can you write it?*
Adrian	(He does write it.) *It's like 'moon'.*
Teacher	*How do you know 'moon'?*
Adrian	*It's like zoo.*

Adrian has discovered how words work.

These three children, who began exploring writing by focusing on marks and shapes and inventing, are well on their way to becoming effective writers of interesting messages.

20 | Summary

Preschool children engage in drawing and writing to share their stories, to play with language and writing materials, to imitate adults, to create personal messages, to communicate with others, and to explore. As the examples in this book show, much happens for young learners when they are encouraged to write. Gradually, they show more competence in writing their messages and stories, and they acquire complex understandings about representing their meanings in written form. They gain awareness of concepts of print including where to start and which way to go when writing a message. Their unique, primitive printing becomes conventional, and their ability to write readable messages, representing the sounds in words correctly, increases.

All of this happens without special instructional attention when children are allowed to write their own meaningful messages. This means they work with many complex aspects of written language simultaneously, and such activity creates the potential for discovery and learning.

Parents, caregivers, and preschool teachers can support and enhance each learner's experiences by allowing children to work on their own time schedules and by praising their efforts. Use the recommendations suggested in this book to engage children in writing and delight in your observations of their discoveries. You are building a strong foundation for literacy together, and you and the children will find satisfaction and excitement in the remarkable pathways to writing that you share.